Excuses, Excuses!

Charles Keller

Illustrated by
Kimble Pendleton Mead

Sterling Publishing Co., Inc.
New York

To Gabriel and Bowen

I would like to acknowledge the help of Steven Blance, Marcus Bocchino, Rhoda Crispell, and Brenda Gordon.

10 9 8 7 6 5 4 3 2 1

Published by Sterling Publishing Company, Inc.
387 Park Avenue South, New York, N.Y. 10016
© 1999 by Charles Keller
Distributed in Canada by Sterling Publishing
% Canadian Manda Group, One Atlantic Avenue, Suite 105
Toronto, Ontario, Canada M6K 3E7
Distributed in Great Britain and Europe by Chris Lloyd
463 Ashley Road, Parkstone, Poole, Dorset, BH14 0AX, England
Distributed in Australia by Capricorn Link (Australia) Pty Ltd.
P.O. Box 6651, Baulkham Hills, Business Centre, NSW 2153, Australia
Manufactured in the United States of America
All rights reserved

Sterling ISBN 0-8069-4460-9

Contents

CHAPTER 1
SORRY ABOUT THAT!

MOTHER: Why didn't you put the dinner dishes in the sink?

DAUGHTER: The breakfast dishes are still there.

MOTHER: Why are you wearing my clothes?

DAUGHTER: They're finally back in style.

MOTHER: Didn't I tell you not to run around with that crowd?

DAUGHTER: That's why we walk.

MOTHER: Why is there a strange baby in the crib?
DAUGHTER: You told me to change the baby.

MOTHER: Why are you standing at the window?
DAUGHTER: You told me I was a pane.

MOTHER: Why are you holding your hands over your mouth?
DAUGHTER: I'm doing what you told me. I'm trying to catch my breath.

MOTHER: Why is the radio on?
DAUGHTER: 'Cause I can't hear it when it's off.

MOTHER: Did you make your bed today?
DAUGHTER: Yes, Mom, but I think it would be easier to buy one.

MOTHER: I just heard a crash in the kitchen. What on earth are you doing?
DAUGHTER: Nothing now. It's done.

MOTHER: Why didn't you tell me your stomach hurt?
DAUGHTER: Aw, Mom, I figured you'd just say I was bellyaching.

TEACHER: How come you didn't touch your school books?
STUDENT: I wanted to keep them in mint condition.

MOTHER: Your homework is all wrong. Didn't your father help you?
CHILD: Yes, and that's why.

PRINCIPAL: Why did you leave class?
STUDENT: The teacher told me it was a pop quiz, so I went home to get my dad.

TEACHER: Why is that piece of cheese near your computer?
STUDENT: I'm trying to attract the mouse.

TEACHER: Why are you students playing soccer with your notebook?
STUDENT: You said we should kick around some ideas.

TEACHER: Why are you copying off Jimmy's paper?
STUDENT: Because he studied.

TEACHER: Why are you carrying a turtle to school?
STUDENT: It would take him forever to walk.

ART TEACHER: Your drawing of the stagecoach is
very good, but what holds it up? It has no wheels.
STUDENT: The bad guys.

TEACHER: Aren't you ashamed to be left back?
STUDENT: No, I'm used to it by now.

TEACHER: How is your son doing in accounting
class in school?
PARENT: Terrific. Now, instead of asking us for his
allowance, he bills us for it.

JUDGE: How can you say this is your first offense?
DEFENDANT: I used an alias the other times.

JUDGE: Why don't you give the money back you stole?
DEFENDANT: I need it for bail.

JUDGE: Are all the statements you made true?
DEFENDANT: All but all the parts I made up.

JUDGE: Why won't you swear to tell the truth?
DEFENDANT: I gave up swearing.

JUDGE: Why won't you testify in your own behalf?
DEFENDANT: Even I wouldn't believe a crook like me.

JUDGE: Why are you defending yourself?
DEFENDANT: My lawyer is in jail.

JUDGE: Why are you here again?
DEFENDANT: I had to steal to pay the last fine.

JUDGE: Is there any reason I shouldn't throw the book at you?
DEFENDANT: Yeah, I stole it the last time I was here.

JUDGE: Why did you leap over the bench and fall on top of me?
DEFENDANT: I wanted to throw myself at the mercy of the court.

JUDGE: Why are you shouting?
LAWYER: You told me you couldn't hear the case.

JUDGE: Why do you break into other people's homes?
DEFENDANT: Because there is too much crime on the streets.

JUDGE: Why did you steal that jewelry?
DEFENDANT: I didn't want to come home empty handed.

CUSTOMER: Why doesn't this restaurant have any specials?
WAITER: Because nothing about this food is special.

CUSTOMER: How come the Board of Health hasn't come in and closed you up?
WAITER: They're afraid to eat here.

PATRON: Didn't you tell me the chef here cooked for the late heads of Europe?
WAITER: Yes, and that's why they are the late heads of Europe.

WAITER: If you know the food here is so lousy, why do you keep coming back?
CUSTOMER: It reminds me of my ex-wife's cooking.

CUSTOMER: Why is this sandwich half eaten?
WAITER: I didn't have time to finish it.

DINER: Why are the waiters in here so nasty?
WAITER: Look at who they have to serve.

PATRON: This bread is stale.
WAITER: It wasn't last week.

CUSTOMER: Waiter, this food is repeating on me.
WAITER: Good, we love repeat business.

WAITER: Why didn't you make all the food on that long order?

COOK: Because I'm a short order cook.

PATRON: Waiter, why is there a spider in my glass?

WAITER: It scares away the flies.

WAITER: Why are you taking so long to order?

DINER: I can't decide whether I want heartburn or nausea.

CUSTOMER: Why don't you eat here, waiter?

WAITER: Serving it is bad enough, I don't want to compound the felony.

DOCTOR: I thought I told you to watch what you eat.

PATIENT: I did, I ate in front of a mirror.

PATIENT: Why did you say I was the picture of health?

DOCTOR: You are, but the frame is bent.

PATIENT: Why did you send someone named William to my house?

DOCTOR: I told you I'd send you a bill.

PATIENT: Why are you washing that piece of paper?

DOCTOR: I wanted to give you a clean bill of health.

DOCTOR: Why don't you stay off your feet?

PATIENT: What am I supposed to do, walk on my hands?

PATIENT: Why does your nurse handle all the needles?

DOCTOR: Because I faint at the sight of blood.

DOCTOR: Do you suffer from arthritis?

PATIENT: Do you know anyone who enjoys it?

DOCTOR: I don't like your test results.

PATIENT: I can't help it. I couldn't study.

PATIENT: Why don't you examine my trunk?

DOCTOR: I'm a doctor, not a tree surgeon.

DOCTOR: Why did you bring a pillow to my office?

PATIENT: Because I'm sick and tired.

PATIENT: Why aren't you worried about my operation?

DOCTOR: Why should I be? I'm not the patient.

DOCTOR: Why did you ask for a second opinion from me?

PATIENT: Because I didn't believe you the first time.

CHAPTER 2
CAUGHT AGAIN!

POLICEMAN: Why are you driving without a license?
MOTORIST: Because it was revoked months ago.

POLICEMAN: How can you say you don't have any
    outstanding tickets?
DRIVER: They're all in the glove compartment.

POLICEMAN: Did you realize you just missed that
    bus with your car?
MOTORIST: Did you want me to hit it?

POLICEMAN: Why didn't you obey that stop sign?
DRIVER: I don't believe everything I read.

POLICEMAN: Didn't you see the signs with the speed limit?

DRIVER: I thought they were just suggestions.

POLICEMAN: Why are you sitting on the sidewalk?

PEDESTRIAN: The sign says "No Standing."

POLICEMAN: Why have you parked your bus here?

BUS DRIVER: The sign says "Bus Stop."

MOTORIST: Why are you crying after giving me that ticket?

POLICEMAN: It was a moving violation.

POLICEMAN: Why were you speeding?

MOTORIST: I was trying to get away from the crime scene.

POLICEMAN: Didn't you see that stop sign?

DRIVER: I keep my eyes closed in traffic.

BOSS: Why didn't you work on the growth chart?
EMPLOYEE: Because I'm not going to grow any taller.

BOSS: Why aren't you ever in the office?
EMPLOYEE: Because you'd find me there.

BOSS: Why don't you invest in the company?
EMPLOYEE: With workers like me you'd never make any money.

WORKER: Why don't you pay me what I'm worth?
BOSS: I don't have any spare change.

BOSS: Why are you against the four day work week?
WORKER: I'm against any week that has work in it.

BOSS: Why do you always have an excuse for everything?
EMPLOYEE: I spend the whole day thinking them up.

BOSS: Why don't you take a vacation?
EMPLOYEE: I've been on one since you hired me.

BOSS: Why are you sleeping in there?
WORKER: They call it the rest room, don't they?

BOSS: Why are you doing your nails?
EMPLOYEE: You told me to do some filing.

BOSS: Why haven't you finished your work?
EMPLOYEE: I'm no slave to management.

BOSS: How come you're never in at the same time twice?

WORKER: I'm no clockwatcher.

BOSS: Why didn't you work on the proposals?

EMPLOYEE: I'm already married.

BOSS: Why don't you want to be employee of the month?

EMPLOYEE: That means I'd have to work for 30 days.

DETECTIVE: Why are you dancing on that utility pole?

SECOND DETECTIVE: I'm wire-tapping the phone.

FIRST DETECTIVE: Why did you wipe off all the evidence?

SECOND DETECTIVE: My mom told me never to leave any fingerprints around.

DETECTIVE: Do you think I should put on the cuffs?

CRIMINAL: Why? You look good in short sleeves.

DETECTIVE: How did you get into counterfeiting?

SUSPECT: I answered an ad that said, "Make money at home."

WARDEN: Why did you try to escape with a pencil in your hand?

PRISONER: I was tired of the pen.

WARDEN: Why did you try to break out of prison?
PRISONER: I had an overdue library book.

GUARD: Why is there a file in the fruit pie you made?
PRISONER: I ran out of apples.

POLICE CHIEF: Why did you ticket the computer?
OFFICER: It was speeding along the information highway.

DETECTIVE: Why did you dump those vegetables on my desk?
SUSPECT: You said it was time to spill the beans.

POLICE CHIEF: Why do you spend all your time trying to hit flies?
OFFICER: You assigned me to the swat team, didn't you?

FIRST DETECTIVE: Why did you bring that side of beef along?
SECOND DETECTIVE: You said we were going on a steakout.

POLICE CHIEF: Why did you tie a rope on that criminal?
OFFICER: You ordered me to get a line on the suspect.

POLICE CHIEF: Why are you putting handcuffs on that building?
OFFICER: I'm making a house arrest.

COACH: Why didn't you swing at any of the balls?
PLAYER: I wanted to go for a walk.

COACH: Why did you leave the building during the game?
PLAYER: You told me to go for an outside shot.

COACH: Why did you bring a broom to the plate?
PLAYER: You told me I was a clean-up hitter.

COACH: Why do you practice running so much?
PLAYER: So I can get off the field before the fans get to me.

COACH: Why didn't you score that second run?
PLAYER: My mom told me you can't go home again.

COACH: Why didn't you catch that high ball?
PLAYER: I'm afraid of flies.

COACH: Why did you drop the ball and start drooling?
PLAYER: You told me to dribble.

COACH: Why did you miss that easy shot?
PLAYER: So I could fit in with the rest of the team.

COACH: Why are you booing your own team?
PLAYER: Because I don't want to show any favorites.

COACH: Why did you walk every batter?
PITCHER: I was working on a no hitter.

COACH: Why aren't you a better player?
PLAYER: Because I'm not on a better team.

COACH: Why are you players leaving? There's still the second half.
PLAYERS: That's why we're leaving.

GENERAL: Why didn't I see you at camouflage training?

SOLDIER: I'm too good at it.

GENERAL: Why were you running away from the battle?

SOLDIER: I was practicing for retreat.

GENERAL: Why didn't you go to target practice?

SOLDIER: I was afraid you'd make me the target.

SERGEANT: Soldier, your bunk is a disgrace.

SOLDIER: I know, but it's the only one you gave me.

CAPTAIN: Why did you volunteer for the undercover assignment?

SOLDIER: I thought it meant I'd be working in bed.

SERGEANT: Why did you run for cover when that star passed by?

SOLDIER: They said it was a shooting star.

SERGEANT: Why didn't you clean up your footlocker?

PRIVATE: You said it was time for mess.

SERGEANT: Why has it taken you all morning to dig a foxhole?

SOLDIER: I couldn't find a fox.

GENERAL: Why are you wearing that bathing suit on duty?

SOLDIER: I've been assigned to the motor pool.

GENERAL: Why didn't you follow the order to charge?

PRIVATE: I don't have any credit cards.

SERGEANT: Are you happy in the army, soldier?

SOLDIER: Yes, sir.

SERGEANT: What were you before you were in the army?

SOLDIER: Much happier.

CHAPTER 3

DON'T BLAME ME!

CHECK-OUT CLERK: Why are you reading that magazine at the check-out line?

SHOPPER: I wouldn't bring trash like that into my house.

GROCER: Why are you drinking that soda you didn't pay for?

SHOPPER: I have to drink something to wash down the donuts.

GROCER: Why are you throwing those vegetables in the air?

SHOPPER: They're for a tossed salad.

STORE CLERK: Why are you wearing a life jacket?

CUSTOMER: I heard about a final sail.

GROCER: Why are you slapping that fish?

SHOPPER: The sign said it was fresh.

GROCER: Why are you breaking that package in half?

SHOPPER: The coupon said 50 percent off.

GROCER: Why are you loitering here?

SHOPPER: I'm waiting for the fruit to ripen.

GROCER: Why are you shoplifting?

SHOPPER: I can't afford to pay these prices.

GROCER: Why are you shoplifting that steak?

SHOPPER: Man does not live by bread alone.

SHOPPER: Why don't you have a one cent sale?

GROCER: Because I don't sell pennies.

GROCER: Why are you shoplifting?

SHOPPER: Because my wife asked me to pick up a few things.

GROCER: Why are you here with a little black book?

BOY: My mother told me to get a few dates.

WIFE: Why did you chase my mother out of the house?

HUSBAND: You told me to drive her home.

WIFE: Why haven't you made plans for vacation?

HUSBAND: Because you'd probably want to come along.

WIFE: Why didn't you clean the bathtub?

HUSBAND: You said you wanted a ring for your birthday.

WIFE: Why are you carrying your golf clubs?

HUSBAND: You said you wanted to go for a drive.

WIFE: Why don't you ever make me breakfast in bed?

HUSBAND: Because I can't get the stove up the stairs.

WIFE: Why do you prefer the TV to me?
HUSBAND: It has a mute button.

WIFE: Why do you keep taking your meals out in the yard?
HUSBAND: I figure they deserve a decent burial.

WIFE: Why did you give me a cemetery plot for my birthday?
HUSBAND: I figured it was something we could both enjoy.

HUSBAND: Why did you ever marry me?
WIFE: I was too ashamed to have you as a date.

WIFE: Why is there lipstick on your collar?
HUSBAND: My secretary has bad aim.

WIFE: You're late! Dinner is ruined!
HUSBAND: At last now you have an excuse.

WIFE: Why don't we ever go to the theater?
HUSBAND: Lincoln did, and look what happened to him.

GIRLFRIEND: Is there such a thing as love at first sight?

BOYFRIEND: There must be, because I'd never have given you a second look.

GIRLFRIEND: Why are you always late for our dates?

BOYFRIEND: I figure that it's less time for us to argue.

BOYFRIEND: Why didn't you give me anything for my birthday?

GIRLFRIEND: You told me to surprise you.

GIRLFRIEND: Why are you tying me to a trailer?

BOYFRIEND: You said you wanted to get hitched.

BOY: Why are you dating a matchbook?

FRIEND: She's my latest flame.

GIRLFRIEND: Why didn't you get me a choker?

BOYFRIEND: Because the police would have traced it back to me.

GIRLFRIEND: Do you think we're a match made in heaven?

BOYFRIEND: We must be. There's no way on earth I'd get stuck with you.

GIRL: How come you broke up with your boyfriend?

FRIEND: Because he ignored me. If there's one thing I can't stand it's ignorance.

BOY: That's the tenth time you've been to the refreshment table.

GIRL: That's all right. I tell everyone I'm getting it for you.

HE: I hoped you liked the dictionary I bought you for your birthday.

SHE: Yes, I just can't find the words to thank you.

BOY: How about a date on Saturday night?

GIRL: I can't see you on Saturday night. I'm expecting a headache.

MOTHER: How can you get the children to play hide-and-seek for hours?
BABYSITTER: Because I don't look for them.

MOTHER: I haven't heard a peep out of the children.
BABYSITTER: That's because they ran away hours ago.

PARENT: Why are you looking under your bed?
CHILD: I was looking to see if I lost any sleep.

MOTHER: Why was the phone busy all night?
BABYSITTER: The fire department put me on hold.

MOTHER: Why were you kissing your boyfriend in front of the children?
BABYSITTER: You said you didn't want them watching TV.

MOTHER: Why is the TV on so loud?
BABYSITTER: It drowns out the crying.

MOTHER: Get your sister's hat out of the mud.
SON: I can't, mom, she's got it strapped too tightly
under her chin.

CUSTOMER: Couldn't you see I was going bald?
BARBER: No, the shine from your head blinded me.

CUSTOMER: Why is my hairline receding?
BARBER: It's not. Your scalp is advancing.

CUSTOMER: Why did you take off so much hair?
BARBER: I didn't, nature beat me to it.

CUSTOMER: Why doesn't my hairline look good?
HAIR STYLIST: It's on the same old head.

JUDGE: Why were you breaking into the car?
DEFENDANT: My family was inside.

JUDGE: Why did you rob people in broad daylight?
DEFENDANT: I'm afraid to go out at night.

JUDGE: Why have you added assault to robbery?
DEFENDANT: It pays to diversify.

JUDGE: Haven't I seen you three times this month?
DEFENDANT: Yes, it's my busy season.

JUDGE: Why did you steal three TV's?
ACCUSED: I specialize in multimedia.

JUDGE: Why did you become a safecracker?
DEFENDANT: You told me to learn a trade.

JUDGE: Why do you keep robbing banks?
ROBBER: Practice makes perfect.

JUDGE: Why don't you give up your life of crime?
DEFENDANT: It's the only thing I'm good at.

JUDGE: Why did you break that parking meter?
DEFENDANT: It said I expired and I wanted to prove
how wrong it was.

JUDGE: Why were you arrested for petty larceny?
DEFENDANT: I've downsized from grand larceny.

DEFENDANT: Why did you order the bailiff to
dangle me outside the window?
JUDGE: I gave you a suspended sentence.

JUDGE: Why do you always mug older people?
ROBBER: Younger ones fight back.

JUDGE: Why won't you tell the court where you hid
the money?
DEFENDANT: What, and let some thief steal it?

CHAPTER 4
CAN'T HELP MYSELF!

POLICE OFFICER: Why are you driving in a bathing suit?

MOTORIST: I'm in a car pool.

POLICEMAN: Why are you driving that car in circles?

DRIVER: I was just going for a little spin.

POLICEMAN: Why did you stop your car, get out, and yell "coward" at the traffic signal?

MOTORIST: The light just turned yellow.

POLICEMAN: Why were you asleep at the wheel?
MOTORIST: Your siren lulled me to sleep.

POLICE OFFICER: Why were you speeding?
WOMEN DRIVER: I was late for traffic school.

POLICEMAN: Why were you speeding?
MOTORIST: I wasn't going to miss seeing myself on "America's Most Wanted."

POLICE OFFICER: Why did you lead me on a five-state chase?
DRIVER: I love to travel.

POLICEMAN: Did you know your vehicle was reported stolen?
MOTORIST: It wasn't when I took it.

POLICEMAN: Didn't you hear my siren?
MOTORIST: Sure, that's why I sped up.

POLICEMAN: Why did your car just spin around in circles?
MOTORIST: I was making a U-turn and changed my mind.

FOREMAN: Why aren't you working fast?
ROAD WORKER: Our sign says: "Slow Men Working."

BOSS: Why did you leave your last job?
APPLICANT: The witness protection program relocated me.

BOSS: Did you take work home?
EMPLOYEE: Why? I don't do any here.

BOSS: Why are you always outside when you should be in here working?
EMPLOYEE: You said it was important to work out.

BOSS: It says on your job application you were a servant in a restricted facility. What does that mean?
APPLICANT: I was serving time.

BOSS: Why are you so early this morning?
WORKER: I'm not. I'm really late for yesterday.

BOSS: Why is your expense account so high?
SALESMAN: I don't want people to think you're cheap.

BOSS: You know there are plenty of people who'd love to have your job.
WORKER: That's because love is blind.

BOSS: Why don't you want to go up the corporate ladder?
EMPLOYEE: I'm afraid of heights.

BOSS: Why do you keep calling in sick?
WORKER: It's my best excuse.

BOSS: Why are you dressed like a cowboy?
WORKER: You said you'd show us the ropes.

FOOTBALL COACH: Why are you lying on the field?
PLAYER: You told me it was our down.

FOOTBALL COACH: Why are you wearing that bag
over your head?
PLAYER: I've been sacked.

COACH: Why did you give the other team our
playbook?
PLAYER: It wasn't doing us any good.

COACH: Why didn't you throw a Hail Mary pass?
PLAYER: It's against my religion.

COACH: Why are you wearing a bib?
PLAYER: You said we'd practice dribbling today.

PLAYER: Why are you mad at me for stealing second base?
COACH: You were on third at the time.

COACH: Why did you walk that player?
PITCHER: I was scared. He had a bat in his hand.

COACH: Why did you hold your nose when the ball came toward you?
PLAYER: It was foul.

UMPIRE: Why did you throw cake dough at me?
BASEBALL PLAYER: You said "Batter up!"

COACH: Why did you tackle the cheerleaders?
PLAYER: It's the only team we can beat.

COACH: Why did you pick up that cheerleader?
PLAYER: The quarterback sent me out for a pass.

COACH: Why are you so sure we're going to lose?
PLAYER: Because the other team showed up.

COACH: Why are you cheering for the other team?
PLAYER: I always root for the winner.

MOTHER: I thought you were saving for a rainy day?
DAUGHTER: Can I help it if the weatherman is wrong?

SON: Why can't I borrow the car?
FATHER: Because your mother won't lend it to me.

FATHER: Why did you chase our dog with a fish hook?
SON: The vet said the dog had worms.

MOTHER: Why did you put that clock in with the dog?
SON: They both had ticks.

FATHER: Why didn't you come when I called?
SON: Then you'd expect me to all the time.

FATHER: Why do you keep putting off the yard work?
SON: I learned from your example.

MOTHER: I'd be ashamed if those were my grades.
SON: Then aren't you glad I get them and not you?

MOTHER: Why is there a goat in the house?
DAUGHTER: You said we needed a nanny.

MOTHER: Why did you put a leash on your brother?

SON: You told me he was in the doghouse.

MOTHER: Why are you wearing your little brother's pajamas?

SON: You told me to sleep tight.

MOTHER: Why are you putting honey on your sister?

DAUGHTER: You said she had hives.

BOX OFFICE CLERK: Young man, I can't sell you a ticket. You should be in school now.

YOUNG CUSTOMER: No, it's all right. I have the measles.

TEACHER: Do you want to wind up in the principal's office?

STUDENT: Of course not, I'm barely qualified to be a student.

TEACHER: What can you tell us about the lost continent?

STUDENT: I swear I never touched it.

MRS. JONES: I heard your son is on the school football team. What position does he play?

MRS. SMITH: I believe he's one of the drawbacks.

FATHER: Aren't you ashamed to be at the bottom of your class of twenty-eight?

SON: Oh, it's not that bad.

FATHER: What do you mean, not that bad?

SON: Suppose there were fifty.

SON: I'm too tired to do my homework tonight.

MOTHER: A little hard work never killed anybody.

SON: Then why should I be the first?

TEACHER: I asked all the dumbbells to stand up, and you're the only one who did. Are you the only dumbbell?

STUDENT: No, but I thought you might be a little lonely standing there all by yourself.

MOTHER: Your report card doesn't look good to me.

SMART ALEX: My grades reflect the shocking inadequacy of the school system.

TEACHER: Where is your homework this morning?

STUDENT: You'll never believe this, but on the way to school I made a paper airplane out of it and someone hijacked it.

TEACHER: Can you tell me what happened in 1492?

STUDENT: I don't know. We live on the tenth floor.

CHAPTER 5
MISHAPS HAPPEN!

JUDGE: Why did you become a cat burglar?
PRISONER: I love animals.

JUDGE: Are you going to confess?
DEFENDANT: No, I'm not religious.

JUDGE: Didn't I sentence your father, too?
PRISONER: Yep, we're a family business.

JUDGE: Why don't you try going straight?
DEFENDANT: It would be bad for my image.

JUDGE: Why do you steal watches?
DEFENDANT: I like to have time on my hands.

JUDGE: Why don't you confess?
DEFENDANT: What, and ruin a perfectly good life of crime?

JUDGE: Why did you steal a washing machine?
DEFENDANT: You told me to clean up my act.

NEW YORK JUDGE: Why did you steal a taxicab?
DEFENDANT: Do you know how hard it is to get a cab in New York?

JUDGE: Why were you carrying a concealed weapon?
DEFENDANT: I didn't want anyone to steal it.

JUDGE: Why are you wanted in three states?
CRIMINAL: I'm a popular guy.

JUDGE: You were associating with a woman who's a known criminal. Do you have an explanation?
PAROLEE: I'm attracted to a woman with convictions.

JUDGE: Why didn't both your witnesses testify?
LAWYER: I thought you didn't like double-talk.

WAITER (serving soup): It looks like rain today.
PATRON: Yes it does, but it smells like soup.

CUSTOMER: Why don't you have doggie bags?
WAITER: That would be cruelty to animals.

CUSTOMER: I didn't order this.
WAITER: I know, but your meal tastes worse.

CUSTOMER: Why doesn't your menu list prices?
WAITER: We didn't want to make you sick before
the food does.

CUSTOMER: Waiter, there's a button in my salad.
WAITER: It must have come off while the salad was
dressing.

CUSTOMER: Waiter, I can't eat this meal.
WAITER: Why not? It looks all right to me.
CUSTOMER: I don't have a fork.

DINER: Waiter, please close the window.
WAITER: Why, is there a draft?
DINER: Yes, it's blown my steak off the plate three
times.

DINER: May I please have a glass of water?
WAITER: Why, are you thirsty?
DINER: No, I want to see if my neck leaks.

CUSTOMER: That crust on the apple pie was too
tough.
WAITER: That wasn't the crust, that was the pie
plate.

CUSTOMER: Why does your sign say "Fine Dining"?
WAITER: We can dream, can't we?

CUSTOMER: Do you have bacon and eggs on the
menu?
WAITER: No, we clean our menus regularly.

LEFTY: I eat at a different restaurant every day.
HEFTY: I don't tip, either.

CUSTOMER: Waiter, look at this chicken! It's nothing
but skin and bones.
WAITER: Would you like the feathers, too?

PATIENT: Why do you think I'll live a long life?
DOCTOR: If I haven't killed you by now, nothing will.

DOCTOR: Why won't you go for X rays?
PATIENT: I don't photograph well.

PATIENT: Why did you charge me a group rate?
PSYCHIATRIST: You've got multiple personalities.

PATIENT: I'm still sick. You told me I was as healthy as a horse.
DOCTOR: What do I know? I'm not a vet.

PATIENT: Why are you examining my pants?
DOCTOR: I think the trouble may be in your jeans.

DOCTOR: Why do you always complain about your medications?
PATIENT: They're as hard to swallow as your bills.

NURSE: Would you like an appointment for next week?

PATIENT: No, I'm sick now.

PATIENT: Doctor, didn't you take an oath to heal the sick?

DOCTOR: Yes, but I'm not a fanatic about it.

DOCTOR: How were those pills I prescribed to improve your memory?

PATIENT: I forgot to take them.

MEDICAL STUDENT: Were you late for surgery yesterday?

SECOND STUDENT: Yes, but I only missed the opening exercise.

POLICEMAN: Why were you driving around in circles and laughing?

MOTORIST: I thought I was on a merry-go-round.

POLICEMAN: Why are you walking sideways down the street?

PEDESTRIAN: It's a sidewalk, isn't it?

POLICEMAN: Why were you speeding?

DRIVER: I didn't want to be late for my trial.

POLICEMAN: Why were you speeding?

MOTORIST: I was trying to get home before I ran out of gas.

POLICEMAN: Why were you speeding when I stopped you?

MOTORIST: So I could race home to get my license and registration.

POLICEMAN: Why didn't you check your speedometer?

DRIVER: It broke when I hit 100.

POLICEMAN: Why did you lead me on a high-speed chase?

MOTORIST: Because you'd catch me on a slow one.

POLICEMAN: Why are you driving on the sidewalk?

MOTORIST: It's too dangerous on the street.

POLICEMAN: Do you know how fast you were going?

MOTORIST: No, you're the one with the radar.

POLICEMAN: Why did you crash into that stop sign?
MOTORIST: I was only following orders.

POLICEMAN: Didn't you see my lights flashing?
MOTORIST: No, I was going faster than the speed of
  light.

POLICEMAN: How can you drive so recklessly?
DRIVER: I have to, this is a getaway car.

POLICEMAN: Why didn't you stop at that red light?
MOTORIST: Then you would have caught up with me.

BOSS: Why are you sleeping at your desk?
EMPLOYEE: It's more comfortable than the filing cabinet.

BOSS: Why is there oil on your arms?
EMPLOYEE: You told me to use a little elbow grease.

EMPLOYEE: Why did you move me up to the fourteenth floor?
BOSS: You said you wanted a raise.

BOSS: Why are you always late for work?
WORKER: I'm the model of consistency.

BOSS: Why are you dressed like a lumberjack?
EMPLOYEE: I heard I was getting the ax today.

BOSS: Aren't you familiar with company policy?
WORKER: No, familiarity breeds contempt.

Boss: Why do you always spend so much time at the water cooler?
Worker: If I didn't I'd have to work.

Boss: Why is your face bandaged?
Worker: You told me to put my nose to the grindstone.

Employee: Why won't you let me take another part-time job?
Boss: You only work part of the time here as it is.

Boss: Why are you throwing those ledgers in the air?
Accountant: You told me to juggle the books.

Boss: Are you afraid of hard work?
Employee: No, I'm afraid of any work.

Nat: Why aren't you working?
Pat: The boss and I had a fight, and he wouldn't take back what he said.
Nat: What did he say?
Pat: "You're fired."

CHAPTER 6

WAY OFF BASE!

MOTHER: Why are you wearing antlers?
SON: The barber said to put some moose in my
   hair.

MOTHER: Why didn't you load the dishwasher?
DAUGHTER: Then I'd have to unload it.

FATHER: Why is the clock facing the wall?
SON: The news said to turn it back.

FATHER: Why did you put gloves and trunks on the
   dog?
SON: The vet said he was a boxer.

FATHER: Why don't you get a haircut?
SON: Why? It will only grow back.

FATHER: Why do I always come home to find you and your sister fighting?
SON: So you'll know you're in the right house.

MOTHER: Why are all those vegetables still on your plate?
DAUGHTER: Because we don't have a dog.

MOTHER: Why did you break your brother's toys?
SON: Because I didn't want to ruin mine.

MOTHER: Why are there muddy footprints on the floor?
SON: Because I can't walk on the ceiling.

SON: Why can't we get a parrot?
FATHER: Because I don't need someone else talking back to me.

FATHER: I don't like the crowd you hang around with.
SON: That's all right. They don't like you either.

JUDGE: I can't understand how your client keeps ending up in prison. He's just a stool pigeon.
LAWYER: He likes to be a jailbird.

JUDGE: Why did you take that TV set from the store?
DEFENDANT: I thought it was okay. The sign said "It's a Steal!"

JUDGE: Why did you dump water on the freshly painted steps?
DEFENDANT: The sign said "Wet Paint."

JUDGE: Why won't you take the oath?
WITNESS: I never swear in public.

JUDGE: Why did you remove the witness chair?
DEFENDANT: You told me to take the stand.

JUDGE: When are you going to stay out of jail?
DEFENDANT: When are you going to stop finding me guilty?

JUDGE: Why did you steal that suit?
DEFENDANT: So I'd look good in court.

JUDGE: Why did you steal that painting?
CRIMINAL: The statue was too heavy.

JUDGE: Why did you steal those hubcaps?
DEFENDANT: The car I stole the day before didn't have any.

JUDGE: Why were you scalping those tickets?
DEFENDANT: I couldn't sit in all of them.

JUDGE: Why is it that you always go free?
DEFENDANT: My lawyer is as big a crook as I am.

JUDGE: Why did you rob the same store twice?
ROBBER: I had double coupons.

JUDGE: Why did you steal the car?
CROOK: I needed it for the getaway.

MOTHER: Why did you get such a low mark on the test?

SON: Because of absence.

MOTHER: You were absent on the day of the test?

SON: No, but the kid who sits next to me was.

TEACHER: Well, at least one good thing I can say about your son.

MOTHER: What's that?

TEACHER: With grades like that, he can't be cheating.

TEACHER: Why did the pioneers go west in covered wagons?

STUDENT: They didn't want to wait 100 years for airplanes.

TEACHER: Why did you sign your paper with an "X"?

STUDENT: With grades like these, would you sign your real name?

TEACHER: Why aren't you doing better in school?

STUDENT: Don't ask me, you're the teacher.

TEACHER: Did you know you spelled all the words wrong?

STUDENT: Wow! And I wasn't even trying!

TEACHER: Why are you working so hard at penmanship?

STUDENT: How else can I learn to write my mother's name?

TEACHER: Don't you ever think about studying?

STUDENT: Yes, and it's the thought that counts.

TEACHER: Why did you hand in your history report so early?

STUDENT: I figured that the longer I waited, the more history there'd be to learn.

TEACHER: Who was responsible for the French and Indian War?

STUDENT: Not me. I didn't know either of them.

TEACHER: How do you explain these failing grades on your report card?

STUDENT: Those two F's are for effort.

TEACHER: If you don't want to learn, why do you come here every day?

STUDENT: It's part of my parole.

CUSTOMER: I thought the meals here were supposed to be like mother used to make.
WAITER: They are. She couldn't cook either.

CUSTOMER: How long must I wait for that turtle soup I ordered?
WAITER: Well, you know how slow turtles are.

PATRON: How come this fly is swimming in my soup?
WAITER: I gave you too much. It should be wading.

CUSTOMER: What is this fly doing in my alphabet soup?
WAITER: Probably learning to read.

PATRON: Hey, there's a fly in my soup!
WAITER: Why are you complaining? Isn't it cooked?

DINER: What's wrong with these eggs I ordered?
WAITER: Don't ask me. I only laid the table.

DINER: There's a dead fly in my soup.
WAITER: I know. It's the heat that kills them.

CUSTOMER: Waiter, I found a hair in my turtle soup.
WAITER: How about that! The turtle and the hare finally got together.

CUSTOMER: There's something wrong with my hot dogs.
WAITER: Sorry, I'm a waiter, not a veterinarian.

CUSTOMER: This fish isn't as good as what I ordered here last month.

WAITER: That's funny. It's from the same fish.

DINER: Could I have a glass of water?

WAITER: To drink?

DINER: No, I want to rinse out a few things.

WAITER: I'm sorry I spilled a glass of water on you.

DINER: That's all right. My suit is too large anyway.

WAITER: I'm sorry to keep you waiting. Your soup will be ready soon.

CUSTOMER: What bait are you using?

WIFE (to husband): Hurry! Wake up! I just heard a mouse squeak.

HUSBAND: What do you want me to do? Oil it?

MAN: Forget your wife. Let's go play golf. What are you, a man or a mouse?

SECOND MAN: I'm a man. My wife is afraid of mice.

WIFE: That woman next door is wearing the same dress as mine.

HUSBAND: I guess that means that you'll want me to buy you another one.

WIFE: Well, it would be cheaper than moving.

WIFE: I went to the doctor's office and he told me I needed a change of climate.

HUSBAND: That's fine. According to the weather bureau, it's coming tomorrow.

HUSBAND: Are you washing your hair?

WIFE: No, I couldn't find a washcloth, so I'm cleaning the sink with my hair.

WOMAN: You're wearing your wedding ring on the wrong finger.

OTHER WOMAN: I know. I married the wrong man.

HUSBAND: What! Another dress? Where will I get the money to pay for it?

WIFE: Darling, you know I'm not nosey.

HIM: Darling, when we get married, do you think you'll be able to live on my salary?

HER: I think so, but what will you live on?

WIFE: You look haggard. Did you have a rough day?

HUSBAND: I'll say. The computer broke down, so we had to think all day.

MAN: Now that you've gotten married you should take out some life insurance.

NEWLYWED: Nah, I don't think my wife will be dangerous.

WIFE (on safari): Yesterday when that lion charged me you ran away and left me. You once told me that you'd face death for me!

HUSBAND: Yes I would, but that lion wasn't dead.

CHAPTER 7
NO HARM DONE!

PATIENT: Hey, that tooth you pulled wasn't the one
I wanted pulled.
DENTIST: Relax, I'm coming to it.

PATIENT: Doc, isn't $50 a lot of money for pulling
one tooth?
DENTIST: Yes, but you yelled so loud you chased
away the other patients.

PATIENT: Doc, what should I do with all the gold
and silver in my mouth?
DENTIST: Don't smile in a bad neighborhood.

DENTIST: Don't worry. I'm painless.
PATIENT: I'm not.

DOCTOR: Did you follow my instructions and drink water 30 minutes before going to bed?
PATIENT: I tried to, Doc. But I got completely full after drinking for ten minutes.

DOCTOR: Are you taking that cough medicine I gave you?
PATIENT: No, I tasted it and decided I'd rather cough.

PATIENT: Doc, I think that I'm an umbrella.
DOCTOR: A cure is possible if you open up.
PATIENT: Why? Is it raining?

DOCTOR: Don't worry. A lot of people talk to themselves.
PATIENT: I know, but I'm such a bore.

NURSE: Why are you drawing circles on that piece of paper?
DOCTOR: I'm making my rounds.

PATIENT: Why is my stomach always upset?
DOCTOR: Look at the person it's attached to.

JUDGE: Why don't you have any character witnesses?

DEFENDANT: They haven't been paroled yet.

JUDGE: Why do you keep coming back to me?

DEFENDANT: I keep getting caught.

JUDGE: Is there any reason I shouldn't send you to jail?

DEFENDANT: Yeah, the place is crawling with criminals.

JUDGE: Are you proud of your criminal record?

DEFENDANT: Well, I don't like to brag.

JUDGE: Why were there so many witnesses to your crime?

CRIMINAL: I do my best work in front of an audience.

JUDGE: You're always seen with known criminals.

DEFENDANT: So are you, but you never get into trouble.

JUDGE: As a perspective juror do you believe in capital punishment?

FEMALE JUROR: No, I do not.

JUDGE: It doesn't matter. In this case a man is accused of losing $200 in a poker game that his wife was saving for a new coat.

FEMALE JUROR: I may be wrong about capital punishment.

JUDGE: You are accused of assault and battery. You hit your neighbor on the head with a flashlight.

DEFENDANT: Your honor, I think the charge should be reduced to simple assault, because in this case the batteries were not included.

TRAFFIC JUDGE: Speeding, eh? How many times have you been before me?

SPEEDER: Never, your Honor. I tried to pass you on the road several times but my car won't go that fast.

JUDGE: Don't you know that crime doesn't pay?

DEFENDANT: Yes, but the hours are good.

JUDGE: Why did you shoot your husband with a bow and arrow?

WOMAN: I didn't want to wake the kids.

DAUGHTER: I will never learn to spell.
MOTHER: Why?
DAUGHTER: The teacher keeps changing the words.

DAUGHTER: My teacher says I should improve my handwriting.
MOTHER: Good idea. Why don't you do it?
DAUGHTER: If I do, she'll find out I can't spell.

MOTHER: I don't think you want me to help you with your homework. You want me to do it all.
DAUGHTER: Well, isn't that education?

PRINCIPAL: Give me three reasons you want to become a teacher.
STUDENT: June, July, and August.

TEACHER: And where were you this past week?
STUDENT: Stop me if you heard this one before.

TEACHER: Why didn't you go to the back of the line like I told you to?
STUDENT: I did, but someone was already there.

TEACHER: How come your math homework is all correct?
STUDENT: Dad is away from home.

STUDENT: I haven't a pen or paper for this test.
TEACHER: What would you call a soldier who went into battle without a gun or ammunition?
STUDENT: An officer.

YOUNG GIRL: I'm sorry, but I can't give back my report card.
TEACHER: Why not?
GIRL: Because of the "A" you gave me in spelling. My mother is still mailing it to all our relatives.

MOTHER: Why did you get such poor marks on your January report card?
SON: You know everything is marked down after the holidays.

MOTHER: My son refuses to study history anymore.
FRIEND: Why?
MOTHER: He claims they can make it faster than he can learn it.

TEACHER: How is it possible for one person to make so many homework mistakes?
STUDENT: It wasn't one person; my mom helped me.

FARMER: Why is the pail empty? Didn't the cow give anything?
SON: Sure. Nine quarts and a kick.

GRANDFATHER: When I was a young man I thought nothing of a ten-mile walk.
GRANDSON: Well, I don't think much of it, either.

JIMBO: My grandfather fought in the World War, and his father fought in the war before that.
JUMBO: Gee, your folks couldn't get along with anybody, could they?

DAUGHTER: Mom just bawled me out for eating with my fingers.
FATHER: Well, you should have known better. It isn't very clean.
DAUGHTER: If the food isn't clean enough to pick up with your fingers, it isn't fit to eat.

MOTHER: Eat your food, dear. Do you know there are thousands of people starving around the world?

SON: Got a stamp?

FATHER: Don't you feel better now that you've gone to the dentist?

SON: Sure do. He wasn't in.

MOTHER: Now remember, when you go to the party, what will you do when you've had enough to eat?

SON: Come home.

FATHER: While you're in the kitchen could you tell me what the big hand is on?

SON: A chocolate chip cookie.

SON: Dad, could I have a bike?

FATHER: You're too old for a bike.

SON: I guess you're right. Make it a car.

SON: Dad, how long will it be before I can do as I please?

FATHER: Son, nobody lives that long.

FATHER: Whose fingerprints are those on the door I just painted?

SON: Not mine, I kick the door when I come in.

SON: Someone told me I looked like you.

DAD: What did you say?

SON: Nothing, he was bigger.

CHAPTER 8
OOPS!

PAL 1: Why are you writing numbers all over my body?

PAL 2: I'm counting on you.

GUEST: Why did you offer me a piece of candy?

HOTEL CLERK: You said you wanted the best suite in the hotel.

GAMBLER 1: Why did you put locks on your sleeves?

GAMBLER 2: I didn't want to lose my shirt.

TEENAGER: I've been shaving now for two years.

FRIEND: Is that true?

TEENAGER: Yeah, I cut myself both times.

EXPERT: I always put my right shoe on first.

NOVICE: Why's that?

EXPERT: It would be dumb to put on the wrong one first.

EXPERT: My dumb cousin has been making chocolate cookies.

NOVICE: How can you tell?

EXPERT: There are M&M shells all over the floor.

DOCTOR: How did you get that big bump on your head?

ATHLETE: From diving.

DOCTOR: Diving? Where?

ATHLETE: In my bathtub.

DIM: Why is there a bookmark in your sandwich?

DUM: It tells me where the meat is.

LOONEY: Are you a regular nuisance?

TOONEY: No, I have other jobs.

LIZZY: Why did you throw your sneakers away?

DIZZY: They kept sticking their tongues out at me.

DIMBO: Oh, no, I forgot to bring my mittens.

DUMBO: Why didn't you tie a string around your finger?

DIMBO: Because a string won't keep my hands warm.

NIT: Can you ice-skate?

WIT: I don't know—I can't stand up long enough to find out.

POLICEMAN: How can you be so sure you were only going 25 miles per hour?
MOTORIST: I was going to the dentist.

POLICEMAN: Didn't you hear me whistle at you?
WOMAN DRIVER: Sure, but I don't flirt when I drive.

POLICEMAN: Are you going to a fire?
MOTORIST: No, I'm trying to prevent one. That's what my boss said would happen if I were late again.

COP: Why didn't you stop when I shouted at you back there?
MOTORIST: I thought you were saying "Good morning, Mr. Mayor."
COP: Right. I wanted to warn you about going too fast through the next town.

POLICEMAN: What do you think you're doing parking your car there?
MOTORIST: I thought it was good place. It says "Safety Zone."

POLICEMAN: What do you think you're doing driving through that intersection fifty miles an hour?
DRIVER: My brakes don't work so I was rushing home before I had an accident.

TEENAGE DRIVER: But, officer, I'm a college man.
POLICEMAN: Sorry, but ignorance is no excuse.

POLICEMAN: I've had my eye on you for some time
now.

YOUNG LADY: That's funny. I thought you were
arresting me for speeding.

POLICEMAN: Hey, you crossed the street when the
sign said "Don't Walk."

PEDESTRIAN: I thought it was an ad for the bus
company.

POLICEMAN: I suppose you're going to tell me you
weren't speeding.

MOTORIST: I was speeding all right, but I was
testing you to see if you were paying attention.

GROCER: Why are you juggling the produce?
SHOPPER: Because I love mixed vegetables.

SHOPPER: Why don't you honor coupons?
GROCER: Why should I? What did they ever do for me?

SHOPPER: How can you sell eggs with a broken shell?
GROCER: I consider them omelets with a head start.

CUSTOMER: You said these pants were pure wool, but the label says "all cotton."
CLERK: Oh, that's just to keep the moths away.

MAN: I'd like a new hat for my wife.
STORE CLERK: Sorry, we don't make exchanges.

CLERK: That suit looks nice. It fits like a bandage.
CUSTOMER: Thanks. I bought it by accident.

CLERK: This jug is genuine Indian pottery.

CUSTOMER: But it says "Made in Cleveland."

CLERK: Haven't you ever heard of the Cleveland Indians?

LADY: I found a fly in one of those raisin buns you sold me yesterday.

BAKER: Bring it back and I'll exchange it for a raisin.

CUSTOMER: How can you make money selling watches so cheaply?

JEWELER: Easy, we make money repairing them.

SHOPPER: This lettuce doesn't have any body to it.

GROCER: That's because we buy it by the head.

CLERK: Would you like to buy a pocket calculator?

CUSTOMER: No, thanks. I know how many pockets I have.

CONDUCTOR: Why do you sometimes wave to the audience during a song?

SINGER: I do that when I hit a hi note.

CONDUCTOR: Why did you hit the music sheet with your violin?

MUSICIAN: You told me to strike the right note.

CONCERT GOER: Why are you sitting on stage near the band?

SECOND CONCERT GOER: You said our seats were in the orchestra.

MINISTER: Why are you tapping on that man?

MUSICIAN: You told me to play a him.

MUSICIAN 1: How did you get the people next door to stop complaining about your violin playing?

MUSICIAN 2: I started playing the drum.

SINGING STUDENT: Do you think I'll be able to do something with my voice?

PROFESSOR: I think it might come in handy in case of a fire.

MUSIC CRITIC: Why didn't you stretch the notes out a little longer?

BAND LEADER: I couldn't. This isn't a rubber band.

MUSIC CRITIC: Are you playing the flute?

MUSICIAN: No, I'm carving my initials into a drum stick.

CLOWN: Why are you wearing such a large shirt?

SECOND CLOWN: I always perform in the big top.

ACTOR: Why do you always get up when the audience applauds?

SECOND ACTOR: To make it a standing ovation.

BOY: Mr. Magic, are you going to pull a rabbit out of your hat?

MAGICIAN: Not today. I just washed my hare and I can't do a thing with it.

BABY RABBIT: Mommy, where did I come from?

MOTHER RABBIT: A magician pulled you out of a hat. Now stop asking stupid questions.

JUDGE: You are accused with stealing watches and jewelry in addition to money.
DEFENDANT: Yes, Your Honor. I think that money alone can't bring happiness.

JUDGE: You robbed a bank of half a million dollars.
DEFENDANT: It was out of desperation, Your Honor. I was hungry.

JUDGE: You committed six burglaries in one week.
DEFENDANT: That's right. If everyone worked as hard as I do we'd be on the road to prosperity.

JUDGE: Stealing a pair of shoes, eh? Weren't you up before me about a year ago on the same charge?
CROOK: Yes, Your Honor. How long do you expect a pair of shoes to last?

EXECUTIONER: What would you like for your last meal?
CONVICT: Mushrooms. I was always afraid to have them before.

LAWYER: As your attorney I'm sorry I couldn't do more for you.
ACCUSED: Thanks. Ten years is plenty.

JUDGE: Don't you ever listen to your conscience?
DEFENDANT: Yes, but I get poor reception.

POLICE CHIEF: Why did you arrest that doctor?
OFFICER: He was trying to take someone's pulse.

CRIMINAL: Why don't you hire these twins for the robbery, boss?

CRIMINAL BOSS: I'm afraid of a double-cross.

VICTIM (to mugger): But my watch isn't any good, it only has sentimental value.

MUGGER: That's all right. I'm sentimental.

CHAPTER 9

MY MISTAKE!

CADDY: Some day you're having. First you sliced the ball into the bushes, then it hooked into a trap. Now you've driven it deep into the woods. I've searched several minutes now and can't find it. Why don't you just use another ball?

GOLFER: No way, that's my lucky ball.

COACH: Do you know why we're feared by all our opponents?

PLAYER: Because we're sore losers.

COACH: Why didn't you listen when I called a down and out?

PLAYER: I thought you were talking about the team.

REFEREE: Why did you suddenly jump out of the ring, go outside, and run to the end of the block?

BOXER: You told me to go to the corner.

MANAGER: Why did you put a metal band on your finger?

BOXER: You told me to get into the ring.

FISHERMAN: You've been watching me fish for over two hours, why don't you try it yourself?

ONLOOKER: Not me! I haven't got the patience.

FISHERMAN: That's the third large fish you've thrown back. Why are you throwing them back?

OTHER FISHERMAN: My frying pan is only nine inches long.

HUNTER: I ran into a huge bear and he charged me.

WOMAN: Good heavens! What did you do?

HUNTER: What else could I do? I paid him.

FIRST HUNTER: It's getting awfully late and dark and we haven't hit anything yet.

SECOND HUNTER: Let's miss two more and then call it a day.

CAMPER: Let's light a fire. It's getting cold.

OTHER CAMPER: These safety matches won't light.

CAMPER: Well, you can't get any safer than that.

PRIEST: Do you say a prayer every night?
BOY: No, my mother says one for me.
PRIEST: What does she say?
BOY: "Thank God he's in bed."

MOTHER: Look at those dirty wrists! Did you wash
    your hands?
SON: Mom, a guy has to stop somewhere.

AUNT: Are your feet still dirty?
NEPHEW: Yes, but I have my shoes on.

GRANDMA: Were you a good girl in church today?
GRANDDAUGHTER: Yes, Granny. A nice man offered
    me a plate of money but I said, "No, thank you."

MOTHER: Your report card is terrible.
DAUGHTER: I know. I wish they had a subject called
    TV.

MOTHER: Charlie, you were supposed to come
    home from the ballgame in one hour.
CHARLIE: Sorry, it wasn't my fault. I tried to steal
    home in the fifth inning but they wouldn't let me.

MOTHER: Eat your spinach; it's good for growing
    children.
JUNIOR: Who wants to grow children?

BOY: Mom, would you rather have me fall out of a tree or tear my pants?

MOTHER: Naturally, I'd rather have you tear your pants.

BOY: Good, your prayers have been answered.

FATHER: You know your problem? You're always wishing for things you don't have.

SON: What else is there to wish for?

TEACHER: This test is multiple choice.
STUDENT: Then I choose not to take it.

COACH: Don't you know the name of the college
you're going to?
ATHLETE: I don't have to. I'm a football player
there.

MOTHER: Your grades are terrible. You have
nothing but C's and D's on your report card.
DAUGHTER: Those aren't grades. They're vitamin
deficiencies.

MOTHER: Were you late for school again?
SON: Yes, but my teacher said it's never too late to
learn.

TEACHER: Why didn't you write your report on vegetables?
STUDENT: I did, but my brother ate it.

MOTHER: Shouldn't you be doing your homework before going to the playground?
SON: That's okay. I'll let it slide.

TEACHER: Who defeated the Philistines?
STUDENT: Sorry, I don't follow the minor leagues.

TEACHER: Why haven't you shown your parents your report card yet?
BILLY: Because I haven't finished making out my will yet.

PETE: Have you kept up with your studies?
REPEAT: Yes, but I haven't passed them yet.

TEACHER: Sarah, you shouldn't laugh aloud in class.
SARAH: Sorry, I smiled and it burst.

MOTHER: You seem to be a bad student at school.
SON: Yes, but I'm a whiz at recess.

MOTHER BANANA: Why didn't you go to school today?
LITTLE BANANA: Because I didn't peel well.

WOMAN: Why are you begging for a quarter?
BUM: I didn't think someone like you would give
me a dollar.

FIRST RANCHER: What's the name of your spread?
SECOND RANCHER: The Double Circle Large
Diamond Ranch.
FIRST RANCHER: How many cattle do you have?
SECOND RANCHER: Only two. Not many survive the
branding.

TOURIST: What's the speed limit in this hick town?
SMALL-TOWNER: We don't have one. You strangers
can't get out of here fast enough for us.

TOURIST: The flies are awfully thick around here.
Don't you ever shoo them?
NATIVE: No, we just let them go barefoot.

FIRST FARMER: I got a job on a farm detasseling corn.

SECOND FARMER: But aren't you allergic to corn?

FIRST FARMER: Yeah, but $8 an hour is nothing to sneeze at.

LION: Why aren't you strong and beautiful like I am?

MOUSE: I've been sick.

FIRST DOG OWNER: My dog has no tail.

SECOND DOG OWNER: Then how do you know when it's happy?

FIRST OWNER: It stops biting me.

MOTHER: Jane, stop making faces at that bulldog.

JANE: Well, he started it.

LITTLE GIRL: Does your dog bite strangers?

DOG OWNER: Only when he doesn't know them.

PUBLISHER: Why don't you drop that piece of wood and finish the book?
WRITER: I can't. It's a writer's block.

EDITOR: How can you paint a true picture of life in Tibet? You've never been there.
WRITER: Neither have my readers.

WRITER: Don't you think I'm the writer of the age?
OTHER WRITER: Yes, six to ten.

NEWS REPORTER: To what do you attribute your old age?
OLD TIMER: To the fact that I was born in 1890.

REPORTER: What made you go out on that dangerous pond ice and risk your life to save a friend?
BOY HERO: I had to do it. He had my skates on.

NEWS ANCHOR: Why are your weather forecasts never right?
WEATHERMAN: I don't want to break my streak.

OUT-OF-TOWNER: What kind of weather did you have yesterday?
LOCAL RESIDENT: I don't know. It was so foggy I couldn't tell.

CAVEMAN: Some crazy weather we're having.
CAVEWOMAN: We never used to have weather like this until they started using those bows and arrows.

NIT: Why do you always answer my question with a question?

WIT: Why not?

OLDER BROTHER: How can you be such a perfect idiot?

YOUNGER BROTHER: I practice a lot watching you.

FLIP: Do you sleep a lot?

FLOP: No, I just lie around with my eyes closed.

TEACHER: How can one person make so many mistakes in a day?

STUDENT: I get up early.

DINER: Waitress, the portions are getting smaller.

WAITER: It's just an optical illusion. It's just that the restaurant has been enlarged.

MOTHER: When you yawn, you're supposed to put your hand over your mouth.

CHILD: What! And get bitten?

RESIDENT (on intercom): Who goes there?

DOORMAN: I don't know. I'm new here.

CUSTOMER: I'd like a watch that tells time.

CLERK: Don't you have a watch that tells time?

CUSTOMER: No, you have to look at it.

SWIMMING INSTRUCTOR: I want you to jump off a 30-foot platform. What would you do if you were on a sinking ship that high?

STUDENT: I'd wait unit it sank another 20 feet.

BANK CUSTOMER: Why did you hit me on the head with that bag of change?

TELLER: You said you wanted your money in a lump sum.

MOTHER: You don't seem to know which side your bread is buttered on.

CHILD: It doesn't matter, I eat both sides.

TENANT: Does the rain always come through the roof like this?

LANDLORD: No, only when it rains.

BOSS: Did you cut yourself?

EMPLOYEE: No, I fell asleep on a chain saw.

MOTHER: Are you washing the dishes?

SON: No, some mosquitoes cursed at me and I'm drowning them.

TOURIST: Is this 99 Main Street?

RESIDENT: No, it's 66, but we turn it upside down to confuse people.

CALM PERSON: Why are you always accusing people of doing things you do?

NERVOUS PERSON: I don't do that, you do.

DRIVER EDUCATION SUDENT: Did you like the way I parked the car?

INSTRUCTOR: It's close enough. We can walk to the curb from here.

MOTORIST: When I bought this car you told me it was rust-free, but underneath it's covered with rust.

DEALER: Yes, sir. The car is rust-free. We didn't charge you for it, did we?

MOTORIST: Does a deer have a horn?

POLICE OFFICER: No, a deer has two horns.

MOTORIST: Then it must have been a car that ran over my uncle.

About the Author

Charles Keller has been working and playing with comedy all his life. Working for CBS as a script consultant, he edited many of the great classic sitcoms, such as *M*A*S*H, All in the Family,* and *The Mary Tyler Moore Show,* and he also worked on other prime-time comedy shows. He got started writing children's books because he didn't like many of the ones he read and thought he could do better. Now, over 50 books later, he maintains the country's largest archive of children's rhymes, riddles, witty sayings, and jokes and constantly updates his massive collection. When he isn't writing children's books, he can be found creating educational software for children. Born in New York, Charles Keller is a graduate of St. Peter's College. He presently resides in Union City, New Jersey.

About the Illustrator

Kimble Pendleton Mead has been drawing funny pictures all his life (despite the efforts of most of his teachers). He lives in Brooklyn and Maui.

INDEX